RIDING THE MAST WHERE IT SWINGS

POEMS by ANNE PAOLUCCI

I wish to thank *Pacific Moana* for permission to include in this volume *Tropic of the Gods* (revised).

"O antique fables! beautiful and bright . . ."

CONTENTS

RIDING THE MAST WHERE IT SWINGS

IF LEAVES COULD HOWL

If leaves could howl
We'd all be deaf by now.
Doesn't take long to never mind
The rain so long as it sweeps us
Into verse. We write best
When complaining. Our flying
Is all vaudeville, feet first,
Even those of us with crowns
All kinds
Frown over breakfast when skin
Is stripped to gold
And trees move out.

SHADOW BOXERS

Tell me about history, you said.
  What do I know about the dead
  Except clippings frayed tan
  Around the edges? Even if I tried
  To read those stained and yellow sheets,
  What would they say to me right now?
  I thought I knew my nose,
  The light thin hairs around my mouth,
  Can I be sure about this face?
What was it like? you asked.
  Am I then? Was I now?
  What I could was in my frown.
Lines are much too short (I said)
To pull in anything. One drowns.
Oh yes, I wore my hair that way.
Drank beer once in a while.
My first manhattan was at a prom
With a boy I hardly knew.
Eight of us at sixteen trying out sin
For size.
Where? When? you pinned me down.
  How can I tell a place that's gone?
  I might have said: You're looking at it
  (What? Where?
  Why, everything that's washed ashore
  Here in my eyes!)
  I could have said: Splinters catch
  The nagging at the core,
  Don't try unraveling.
  I might have said: It's up to you

12

To try the door.
I never heard it close before.

GARRAN HALL

Lovely parrot lady quick and small
Full of talk
Large in your wing
When you felt ripe and tall,
The drive into weekend places
Was vintage. I learned to read
Your hands on the wheel,
Drumming the chair too large
For tired evenings
You took flight. Some wine
Helped, the Indian sculpture
Had a friendly look.
You hosed down treasures,
Willed flowers out of the ground.

POETS OVER THE SINK

"Sister Death!" he cried with his last breath—
"God-goodness knows no bounds
It shapes the sounds we make
To match the blueprint of his mind!"
Is shouting enough?
Caught in overripe gardens
What sort of fig leaf do we fashion
For our secret places?
Briefly we hide from our own swift lancers
Created in the image of our answers.
No telltale smells to flush out cancers.

Vigil by night, the final bluff.
Flies drown in water glasses
Filled in our bloated mercy for the dying.

THE OPERA HOUSE
(FOR NEAL, IN SYDNEY)

Rain charged with pellets of cold
Hammered us to the water's edge
For cover. All other sap
Drained into the smell of sea.
We fingered oranges pears
Bought macadamia nuts.
Against the wind white-peeled
Ready to drop anchor
I wondered at the bridge so long in faith
Tried the wetness where it lapped
The music in me still untapped.

AT THE AIRPORT

Hard to miss eight in the morning
Sipping gin. We said goodbye
At the bar. I wore large things
What I couldn't squeeze into my bag.
You came in a sweat shirt
Cleared the table where we sat.
Is there room in one life
For so much cluttered space?

LOOKING FOR THE RIGHT TREE

It's not easy to plant your body
When a dog's around.
He sniffs the scent above the ground.
He can with purpose feast on air.

If a dog's around
He'll teach you how to bark,
Show you forgotten tracks
Lead you to his family of trees.
He'll teach you how to bury sounds
In the wind.

SYBIL

She said she'd talked to God that day
(He too got drenched walking in the rain
Even in his cloud of fire)

Not enough (I thought unkindly)
To prevent your catching cold.
She said he cried, told her she was saved.
I watched her glow.
She said he touched her (like this)
Her hair turned gold.

I thought: blondes have all the fun.
She tried to sell me orgiastic prayer
All that happened was I burned the bread
My kitchen choking with her smell.

I thought: saints stumble into others' hell
And come out grinning. What damn luck!
They don't cook, grow old.

PALLONE LUNA!

Pallone moon! Bloated pink and tourmaline
Daydreams rising from the heat of lust—
Some day I'll find proper words
What poets say about such things,
About perfect look when fragile
You sweep up horizons.

Meantime I wonder at your colors
How you come to rest
At white to rust
On lamp posts on the bridge
A huge lollipop

I lick my fancies
In all flavors

I like you best that way.

PETRARCH AT VALCHIUSA

When the dying animal in his care
Fled Florence, weary in transparencies,
Then Venice to Valchiusa where he hoarded
Time for release,
The old man would start up dusty with sleep
And scribble in the dark
Conjuring magnificent ghosts on Roman hills
Ready for martyrdom and transfigurations.
Their pity cowls the night.
We brush against receding lines
Perfect-bound in our arrogant intrusion.

Shall we weep sing swoop?
Grow or wilt? Never droop carping
About greatness. Not to brood!
Says my carrara angel
Hugging his tiny foot
Trying on his navel. I trust him.
He taught me plants. In my garden
We read silence into the earth.

DORA

Large in the right floppy hat
First woman. She gave birth
To poplars. Sheen enough!
A porcelain brotherhood gleams
Smugly from an antique shelf.
Over a low flame
In the Cafe do Brazil
Lazarus stirs.

Many times once we walked the Vomero
To sip thick afternoons
Arm in arm through Etruscan silences,
Ruins that will not crumble.
We searched for small gods
Paper pagodas. Geraniums
Gave us courage.

SUMMER SOLSTICE

Somebody's pearls scatter
As I nibble scraps of toast,
Patterns rise in the dust.
At midnight my neighbor strolls out
On his balcony in shorts
To play his violin.
I turn cello, watching him.
In the spring, some kind of tuning
For the soul. Now, poised
In transubstantiation, I drowse
My glasses still on.
I dream better, I think.

THE PASSION ACCORDING TO

And he wept bitterly till the long look
Of Christ seared his eyes and burned his gold,
Scattering peace to the devil wind.
Lots were cast in the seamless dust
And as luck would have it
Peter won.

And Jesus said:
All bets are closed,
No use hanging around.
He cut Judas from the tree.
Their shadows leaped from the ground
Grew together into a single sound.

RIDING THE MAST WHERE IT SWINGS

Most of my friends are dead,
Those who find my garden like millions of seeds
For a single tree sprout salad leaves
At best, as they strip the ground of pleasure
And turn with the waiting soil to sow
Sun in summer. A few come up
In my window box, caught between
Rhinoceros (how will I ever get them out?),
I try prophecy of red tiles neatly rounded
Around my neighbor's lawn. Their Children
Wave me on, teach me to shout
Whatever ditty seasons bring.
I talk to Milton as I work.
He needs no cue.
I've wondered about Shakespeare too.
Did he join his actors at the Arden bar
When nothing grew enough to brood
Acorns in their pot of gold
And flags flew tired in the wind?

SOUR GRAPES

Some paint their mirrors kind. I,
Like Brutus on the hill, stab badly.
My lady of the images stumbles
On the stairs, climbs, falls again.
What did you have in mind?
Even this place is hard to find!
In his cage, exorcised,
My parakeet turns columbine.

ON THE ROCKS IN SYDNEY

All day you guzzled beer. The bar
Was panelled oak, smooth to lean on.
In the patio the tree bent to small leaves
While we stretched across the Gap
As far as the ringing in our ears could take us
Out to ships resting on a Sunday horizon.
Children screamed water to its crest.
Clouds were thick in my throat.
I liked you
With the sun shining.

ELECTRONIC COMPOSITION

Macadam calls for maps, I said.
Ragged left to some alignment on the right.
Lesser prophets code no-print.

What other options?
How many Serbians have staged
Some Turkish delight? Who the hell
Is Gokalp? How do we brush away
Spots in the sun?
Sure you can rake skulls for new planting,
Scratch warm evenings where they itch,
That and Vondel.
Is it really nobler in the mind?

VIRILITY
(FOR SYLVIA PLATH)

Rage wastes us how we look
Still numb at birth.
Between trips to the bathroom
We shape the fetus of some rape.
Call it love
When all the oracles are cheat or dumb.

Until so many toenails fashioned
This one claw
I dreaded halo hunters.
Their guns rode happy chase
In search of target space.
Then came true believers
Tracking down their own sweet smell.
Eight billion years too late to answer back
I crawl toward the silence in the earth.

ORIGIN OF THE SPECIOUS

You must have noticed how great-aunts
Pin God down mid-air
Sheltered from his wrath
By the hats they wear.
They have a certain flair
For catching flies too.
A noble madness seizes them
When winter lifts their shadow
And they glow Chinese.
Like poets who write best at birth,
Catching what's left of some eternity
In one huge breath,
They pledge us to familiar seasons
Gracious in their own kind treason.
We stand beside them to admire trees.

In the end we marry skinny angels
And sit on chairs resting on casters
On squeaky clean hassocks
Covered with transparent plastic.
Impaled on points of no dimension
We dance to canned laughter.

THE SHORT SEASON
(FOR LUCIA B.)

Almost Homeric
The cherub of my seismographic birth—
Such a big quill in his plump hand!
Everything suddenly so fused and still!
Not yet rheumatic
Barely a puff of grace his wings,
Long before the settling in the earth
The elegance of skill
Later the arrogance of art.

THE TIME OF THE GREAT HORN
(A NARRATIVE FUGUE)

Allegro con brio

Meriwell told me about it
On our last flight to Caracas
Before he retired to Camden.
I knew he lived crazy
Dizzy days sallow with ringed women
Jangling lust in the grass
When drives were cool
And four of us would pull up
On the beach or if it rained
Into a corner of the back seat
A week dead from the *Times*
All right too—
We drank the light blind
Stripped and raped the night
Spreadeagled on sands where nothing grew
Except dead fish crushed shells
Under the weight of strangers—

Told me the old man cursed when I laughed
Never forgave me (he said). Who cares?
I watched the new girls pushing their way
To the bar. Tierney was with me then,
Smoked his cigars told dirty jokes.
The old man sat and listened
Mumbling something about hearing
The ring the hum the thing
Clear as a bell
All the way from hell. I said:

Bells don't hum. It's your head.
I said: Is there another hell
We don't know about?
Sure we laughed
All through that gin night
—Short enough, I said,
And involuted as allegories go.
(How was I to know?)

Largo

The ceiling fans buzzed cut
Dim strips into the light
A breath wide, just enough
To curl around the sides of vision.
In the heat intentions grew limp.
I bought Cecile a drink
Sized up her pimp (a bull-necked Cuban
With cracked teeth)
—Latermaybe, I said, looking
For something firm and fresh,
Cecile was too familiar ground
All those tiny wrinkles stretching
Her mouth wide for cursing.
I craved surprise. Tierney whispered:
The old man went to pack his gear.
I laughed with Meriwell
To the point of tears. Later,
Dreamless in some kind of sleep
I groaned I think. Morning
Oozed a slimy band of light
Through broken blinds,

Cut me thin
At first a low wail not quite a sound—

Andante (crescendo)

Nights are cold here.
Snow buries winds from the south.
Spring is hard. Nerves grow taut
When the ground thaws.
Across the way Van Huser's windows
Cast long shadows where I sit . . . .
Down the hall glasses clink
Make me sweat. I drink the day soggy.
I hear them laughing in the wall
That's the worst time of all . . . .
See how many cracks I've filled?
Winter is best. Snow freezes the earth
Buries the sound where the old man
Left it for me to find.

RETROSPECTIVES

Out of my once removed flesh
You turn down corners,
I recognize sharp edges in your voice.
Born to others you nestle
In my tone and pitch,
Some kind of blood runs through
Our love our anger,
You like my nose,
I touch your hair.

Sometimes I feel my own urgent claims
In your look,
Whatever else we say.
Sometimes I'm young and you seem old,
Tricks that fancy plays—
Kindly you listen how we move
Through labyrinths not realizing
How imperceptibly
We grow into contemporaries.

FROM THE EAST

Is art really better
Than tattered clothes upon a stick?
No golden bird will ever sing
An arc some early spring—
Short seasons give us back
Images
Swooping the sound of wings—

And when we touch ground
The earth is sweet
Where it rises to our breath.

REPORT TO THE ACADEMY

I sit on the bowl smoking.
Outside my poodle
Curious about the privacy of trees
Teaches me to bark
In celebration of new leaves.
I learn to rake them
To his own brand of revelation.

Conquerors both
We lift our ears to recognition
Impassively dismiss the sky.
The frayed and tattered tassels
Of my cotton robe
Sweep our vulnerable eternity
Into the groaning of the earth.
Rain scratches us back to autumn.

D * O * A *

He woke with a start, still dreaming
Of gates that clanged upon his sleep
When darkness flung his body where it lay
Propped against so many splintered crates
Where memory was recent pain.
A voice switched off the light
And he had hurried through the rite
Marvelling at so much sun that bled
And poured its pool inside his head.

No regrets, she said. Afterwards
Her voice spread like a stain
Over the empty room into the hall
On to grass that grew red—
All she really wanted was the smell of bread.
She reached for sleep when all she craved
Was her own familiar bed.
She watched friends file past slowly full of dread
Searching for the place where she had bled,
They genuflected at her feet and head
Fingered the wings that she had shed,
She touched their grief as they were led
Through labyrinths to where she'd fled
Startled by the language of the dead.

AT THE PODIUM

My groggy angels stride bravely
Into Joyce, a little wide of the mark.
Hardly news! I bless the crackling
In their heads, break bread.
I say: Poetry is not too different
From the *New York Times*—
It's just that morning feasts
Rarely fit our rhymes!
After a while they learn to sit
Patiently
For me to smile.

TROPIC OF THE GODS
(FOR MY AUSTRALIAN FRIENDS)

> *"Whatever is hung to dry*
> *Beneath the Southern stars*
> *Is Orient behind a scrim.*
> *There are no tides*
> *When standing still."*

BOOK ONE: *The Limbo Crowd*

On a spit all clouds turn slow.
They too keep going where it's dry.
Southern windows frame our parrot cry
"Acoond is dead, long live Acoond!"
Once in the Bush you steel your head
Or bury it in sand. It grows square.
No need for feet or beds
When Kelly's out there
Training acrobats.

So much for the rules, I said.
You cheat all the time, every game.
The cards always stack up the same—
And when my money was all gone
I pawned a pack of lies:

They carried him on a stretcher
The length of Swat. Shaky still
He got up: —Theirs the deceit,
Who tempted us with their attempt!
Are we going to stand for that?
Listen, confusion can be turned

40

To art, music,
Light planted in profusion
And every broken part rewired
With a new thing called technology. . . .

His eyes grew white inside the hollow
Of his head. He gurgled more
Until in mercy we pronounced him dead.
Kelly presided at the eulogy:
—Flies at war for territory
Swoop over my big toe. What map,
I wonder, brought them to such feast?
Are wings a special treat,
Gods as wanton boys?

BOOK TWO: *Poets in Their Space*

1. Epic Blueprint

All shores rest here. On this side
Monuments of intellect carved whole,
Entrails of great events
Strewn along the waters' edge
Where they dream future seas—
Thames, Arno, Tiber, and Potomac
All trimmed in the beginning
Ocean purpose. Temples rise to spoil
The view: Nails and bones
And building noises shape history
When new. Later, stress and lines,
Tombs of glory. In the beginning,
Temples suffer cranes against their sides,

Agonies of placques and artifacts
Inscribed to honor such a proper shrine.

2. *Lyric Voices Overheard*

Eyes turn Egyptian to mosaics, even when blood
Runs semitic. The feel of fingertips on silk
Is the quality of sphinx in wide repose.
Scholarship is cheap in the houses
Of the dead. So many fragments
Chips of drinking bowls
Depressions in the stone
Bridge puzzles.
Here are the holes where water flowed
To mix the dyes. Even writers like to pose
Against the ruins of Tyre.
Where it fell there are no rules. . . .
Through open windows where we sit
Tracking deserts suddenly there's welcome
Rain. I watch her lips curl
Into hieroglyphics
A kind of mummy in her face.

Body merging is paradox
Silly too.
One wonders at the locks.
Or eucalyptus on Tuscan hills
Transplanted in this time.
Giotto's tower on Black Mountain
Challenges our shock.
Why is the poet's grace so hard?
God hides his face, it's true,

42

But then he taps us on the shoulder
From behind.

3. *Happenings*

Huge globes all in a row
For a bowling tournament of giants.
Constellations walk round and round.
I sit sipping tea, resisting temptation
To follow my own footsteps where they grow
Up there in the snow.
The Southern stars had followed me instead
Across the sea.
I never thought they're reach in here
To crowd us in this reading room
Where tired scholars shape huge myths,
Dive for pearls, rape locks,
Map such oceans as invite
New sails new prows.

—The spheres above the moon
(Said Galileo to the Grand Acoond)
And those below as well
Have all been plotted, Your Exalted Grace!
All that's left to do
Is roll ourselves into position
And kick the ball.
You'll see how Aristotle lied!. . . .
I felt my head begin to spin
Grow dizzy as rectilinear intentions
Took shapes hyperbolic. A voice
Boomed somewhere not too far:

43

—I don't need telescopes
To tell me ships still need
A Ptolemaic sky to sail! I'll nominate
You for the Nobel Prize,
But don't come back
Until you have some better proof!
Even Copernicus knew that!

4. The Bound Volume

When God Almighty scooped up
All his lovely sounds
And buried them in pitted sands,
Our fathers marked and labeled every spot,
Aristotle into Eliot from Pound.
They laminated works-in-progress
And catalogued the tapes
That stored the peeling corners of our age.
They taught us how to stretch a page
To some approximation
Revelation
Differential
Always closer to some mark.
If calculus is true, somewhere
Surely distances no longer split in two
Where waters slice them holy.
Mirrors too tell us how to catch us spying
When we measure noses. Quiddity
May tell us why
Once we cap the sky;
Meantime, left lying about like this,
Words pollute the air—

And storage space is growing every day
More rare.

Afterword

Shadow says
Poem might be
Some morning when pilgrim birds
Congregate to chirp their trellis gods
To speed them flying time
(Enough to wing by when the north whips
Fledglings in the wind).
Slower creatures shuffle into paradox
And sound—as every true Euridyce,
Bird-watcher, Enobarbus knows
Who tries to catch the singing in the ground.

BOOK THREE: The Great Rose in the Middle

1. In the Waiting Room

On the table scrubbed of fingerprints
And stains, I put down my U.S. bottle
Of Liquid Palmolive, open assorted Wrigleys
And fill a bowl with green and yellow wrappers,
Friends from home.
I rearrange the bookcase and chairs
To suit my floating mood, hide bags that brought me
Different here. I have no mirror yet to tell me
If I've grown, even my face is not my own.
Curious neighbors wait for signs
While I sleep.

"There was a birth (that's settled,
You'll agree?) with all its smells
Of creature-incense, mountains
In the distance, and something compelling
Close by. Dusty with dreams
Strangers wondered at my case
Puzzled about crown and mace.
Another race, not mine, though vectors
Soon would cross. Meantime,
I gather loss, sift gain."

Out of vision I switch on shapes
For humming,
There's a buzzing against my lids.
A beetle focuses my will—
If only I had purpose,
Art
Tiny wings!

My last cigarette goes untouched
Each minute grows stale
With my resolve. I wait for it to crumble
Even offer it to colleagues
Who in kindness will not let me part with it.
Reading late at night
I trace its seductive length
Across each line of print
A marker of my will. I reach
The bottom of the page, perversely
Pick up a match. . . .
Friendly enemies in season
Bursting on the vine,

One of us will soon be ripe,
Bruised to give up reason.

Never once doubting small intentions
And final cause are one sublime projection,
My orange peeps over the bowl's rim
Seeking its horizon.
I've scheduled its transfiguration
To my taste my time and pleasure.
Why let analogies destroy the mind?
God grew the perfect fruit,
There's not sufficient proof to say
It's mine, to cling unwilling to be stripped
For his rich wine.

2. *Heart of Darkness*

Rough-shod
Poets step into words
To scramble up epiphanies.
Lemons and melons float across their bliss.
They scoop up moons sometimes
To serve as delicate conclusions.
Is the kink in the sky? Such a tiny cloud
For testing pirouettes! How do I stand?
What do you think about my arms?
How far to the edge can I dance
Without damaging the wiring in my wings?
Unfurled, what do I spell?
Even dogs curl up gracefully
Beside familiar chairs
(Their floor has nothing new to tell

That hasn't been divined before)
And sages dance on coals
Singing litanies on fierce beds of faith.
Ripe to touch, the poet's ritual
Turns every pumpkin from the literal
(For even drunk he's licensed to perform).
Children then take courage
Ride happy such monsters
Where gates are wide into open country,
Mountains brooding on every side
Until the gift of ocean
Where thieves and lovers fold winds
Raise anchor
Follow in their wake.

"Try me, my dancing colors!
My will seized snow and emerald and ruby
To reap a poem out of chaos!
All in due course its place,
Although strength grows less
With each word, and every sound
Eludes me in the shaping. Climbing
The beast's back turned smooth as ice
I felt panic, the smell of death
Thick in my nostrils, jungle flight,
Swift, silent, gaining still,
Stone country without wind or thunder,
Out of bounds. And yet, all the while,
I stood quite still, rooted to the spot,
My blood screaming
Against the abandoned vault
That was my heart

—Escape to what? Even my vivid certainty
Toward light now fails,
And with it the last vestige
Of intention (once crowned and mitred
To officiate at such a feast as this),
Beauty, skill with words. . . .
That part is done.
To become is just another tongue.
I ask nothing. Oblivion is large silence
Beyond art."

THE IDES OF MARCH
(FOR THOMAS BERGIN)

In a sari I might sweep up into
A gift of tongues
(One small word to dramatize
Purpose!)

In a paper skiff
I drift reckless aimless into oceans—

Tell me, you who are my friend:
Is it better to stand each morning
On the edge of the sun bent to purpose?
Once I was patient for large changes
Later it was grace to count stars
Trace patterns in my palm.
Tell me, you who are my guide:
Will it ever be our kind of light
Where forests end and beasts turn back?
I don't mind growing old
But tell me, you who are so bold:
Is shipwreck such a horror really
When your shadow has leaped
Into the sea
And the terror in you
Is stranded on the shore?

THE BLACK HOLE

Behind every door
Acorns swamps Arab Jew
If high enough above
A balcony will do

Cows audition for the part
In Calcutta
Feel sorry for them too

And roaches who clean up
After us when we're through.

FINDING THE RIGHT GIFT FOR N. P.

Without a beard you look vulnerable,
As indeed you are;
With it, you travel to places where disguise
Is pain. Either way, the oaf in you
Peeps through while we judge smiling,
Smile as we judge
(Two very different things that add up
To what *we* are, not you!)—
Constant, summer star on balconies,
You talk lazy, forever new to headaches,
Fears, counter-plots;
You want and not want thinly, with wide banter,
Those things that fill your days to straining.

I wish you a heaven of shish-kabab just right,
Children who tell you everything,
Friends who shrug off your imperfections
Even as they tell you what you are,
Mothers who are kind.
But, you have all that already, don't you,
So I wish you sold-out Passion plays
Among whatever gods there are
In certain realms of perfect coffee
Newly ground, made with spring water
From plastic gallons, in pyrex pots.

REGINA

Jocasta keeps leaving messages.
She shuffles back and forth
Whispers in my ear: All men
At some time dream
Of sleeping with their mothers,
Even Freud knew that!

The rest of us try chorus for size
Make noises in retreat,
When the orchestra starts up
We turn robot with the beat.
She knew ahead of time
What was coming, filled in
What others forgot.

Still-life tells us who at best we are.
It takes at least as long as art.

BIRTHDAY GIRL

Were you happy with shawls and egg holders
Golden heirloom rings for pierced ears?
When you smiled
I tried for all those things I couldn't find,
I heard some kind of stifled cry
The smell of it
Caught me by surprise.

Oh happy deities in niches, dreams!
So many faces still unshaped
So many eyes without a point
To fix on! Shall I scold you
As you walk barefooted on Persian rugs?
This night, first breath of Spring,
Was unpremeditated gift!
By the sink
I willed you slim in blue
Some kind of virgin birth.

SLOW DANCE IN MY HEAD

A child in a striped muffler runs out
Into the snow to try his grace.
He stakes his claim
Impatient for flags.
Later his space, the gentle grief
Of place will tell him about
Trees in the making.

Connecticut turns sullen in its shroud.
While I sleep my neighbor, lord of the tower,
Shovels out his jeep.

Acorns brooding oaks.
Maybe it's just a hoax.
Sweet nutty faces tell me they're my folks.

DEARLY BELOVED

What life so finely tuned is orchestrated
To so fierce a death? We talked once
Briefly on the train.
Sounds break measure sky-change,
The golf cap purple on his head.
Embarrassment becomes obscene
A kind of worship.
Red and yellow lights flash in a circle
As we hover for a blessing,
Something to haunt by.

REDUCTION "AD NOESIS NOESEOS NOESIS"

I thought I knew what makes water arch
Flow fling spray on the tortured shore
Made barren with the shape of flight,
Like the joy of print
Before we learn to write.

I wonder wide at the view
(We all do). Like untried birds
Our best intentions are eager
For the feel of air. Words too.
They track currents gracefully
Into their channel or rush
Into flight. I thought I knew.

In the morning I try again
The letters of my alphabet
Against trapped voices clogging up my mind.
By noon my tired colors drain
Into cloaca maxima with all
That was there spoken.
At night I strain for the single stroke:
He is. They are. I am.
In sleep a slow barge shows me
How to turn into the Bay.
I thought I knew the way.

UNINVITED GUEST

You were on horseback
Straddling the flanks of your own Gothic
Pride. I thought of Caesar
Stretched across a water bed,
I even tried to reconstruct
The time the place the season's worth
Kindly to some stoic birth.
Together we conspired to your sainthood.
Was it, when you crushed the earth?

DA CAPO (WITH SOME FEELING)

I trip over pebbles
Drink Brim-oceans in a tiny cup.
My body, not yours, faltered in the tension
For some new dimension.
You go disco-dancing instead.
So many vessels to measure by!
Pleasure bars our wit.
Once we talked about the shape of art
(Over Taiwan lamps) down to the wick.
You were generous, exotic,
Touched me and I flowered.
Tyrant puppy to small running feet
You scolded clouds.
I grew gentle, capable,
Gathered sermons for a feast,
God was a woman and I stored
Her strength for a treat.

SKIRMISHES

My sweater rough and baggy covered the place
Where your eyes once unraveled me
Tore into my flesh. Am I in my breasts?
Does it show? Artists and lovers can.
Fingers steal upon my ground
Into a field of treasures mined
To blow up as we cross equators
At my waist.
What shall I wear
To tell you who I am?

BETWEEN THE LINES

I feel Black once in a while,
Think Australian, act out plays
In Arabic, profess a commitment
To Scandinavian translations.
I read books backwards at times,
Looking for mystic correspondences.
I've marked the line where
Dante looks behind before going on
In the real journey from the poem's
Beginning to its end.
Stars give us our position on poetic charts.
I've played bit parts in large spectaculars
With Kissinger directing from the wings,
Even though politics is not my thing.

Best is the barking of my dogs
(A language not yet mastered),
I feel them trying out metaphors
With their ears, sniffing inspiration
Buried in the ground—
I don't worry any more about oral literatures
That have no alphabets.

IN THE GREEN ROOM

In the green room my splintered self
Drinks coffee in separate cups,
Dozens of eyes turn expectantly
As I walk through the door.
Voices pitched to parts
Once pleasing in the doing
Greet me. I lean on my umbrella
Stare at the puddle at my feet.
They know their power, rule me
With splendid anticipation,
Wrap me in their feast.
I watch them circle to a new
Beginning, not mine.

ANOTHER GARDEN

In the morning rush of air
I draw purpose deep into my lungs,
Jog standing by the sink,
Arrange colors for my day.
Intentions sprout early looks to some plan.
I try the earth
Push down space firmly around time,
Water tiny points of light
Where beginnings are all about.
My leaves, tentative and shy, turn brown
Around the edges
When you cry.

CONTRAPPUNTO

1. Piatto del giorno

Sì, grazie! un misto d'assurdini
Bolliti in vino
Con fegatini a lutto
Tagliati fini fini.

Dio li benedica! Ancora a pranzo?
Piatti caldi freddi rotti
Ospiti esauriti dotti
Mesti sotto lumini perpetui
Fin da ieri sera—
Tutto insomma come si deve
Dall'antipasto alle candele,
Ed il dolce nuovo servito a letto
Cassata pettoperla meringhiata
Nella nottata con baci
Poi prima di dormire, nello scuro,
Una voglia matta per l'insalatina a taglio—

Che sogno! Sarà l'insomnia sotterrata
Che di mattina vien fuori col prurito
Con quei maledetti gatti!
Sul muro del giardino dove fanno a gara
Nel loro filosofare
Discutendo della prosa:
Se si presta o no
Alla non-poesia, non-arte.

COUNTERPOINT

1. Today's Special

A stew of scattered wits
Might be nice simmered in wine
With chicken livers on the side
Sliced very fine.

Good lord! Still eating?
Since last night cold and hot
And broken dishes
Important visitors exhausted
By their vigil in the flickering lamps—
Everything in place, just right,
From snacks to candlelight,
And now, the new dessert
Served up in bed:
A delicate meringue concoction
Topped with melting kisses in the night,
Then, just before sleep, in the dark,
All the crisp green salad you could want—

An incubus! that buried with insomnia,
Rears up in the morning, that kind of itch,
Cats competing for their place and pitch
On top the garden wall outside
Debating whether prose lends itself or not
To non-poetry, non-art.

2. *Un'altra specie di "requiem"*

Inconsolabili
L'ente, i soci, figli e nipotini,
Le donne tutte
In chiesa presto la mattina
Affrante dal dolore
Per il babbo (ma chè!)
Lo zio (—no. . .)
Il nonnino (e sù, via!)
L'amico—
Insomma, l'inestimabile Signor Padrone.
Ne danno il triste annunzio
Un sacco di brava gente;
Lutto grave poi in ufficina
Dove andava per la benzina. Già,
C'era quella tale. . . Lina. . .
(Basta, meglio non parlare
Che la Signora, poverina—)
Lei, però, ferma sull'uscio del botteghino
Guarda il corteo che s'avvicina.
Gli eredi con nasi afflitti
Passano in nero fitto.
Soltanto quella piccina indiavolata
La prelibata del nonnino
Alza la testina e chiama
Alla signorina, additando la bara:
—Torniamo subito carina!
Lo zio Emilio la tira via
Con la promessa di un gelatino
Alla fine della gita.
Messa solenne pien di sole

2. Another Kind of "Requiem"

Grief-stricken
The entire firm partners sons nephews,
In the morning the women
Are in church bright and early
Crushed by the loss
Of Dear Old Dad (go on!)
Uncle Ben (—no. . .)
Grandpa (oh, come on!)
Everyone's best friend
That paragon of men, Buddy Mr. Great.
So nice so many people
Bought obit space,
In the station where he used to stop for gas
Everyone is deep in black. Well, yes,
There was that girl. . . Lina. . .
(Let's not bring that up, not now
With his poor wife right here—)
She watches the cortege go by
From the doorway,
One by one the family goes past
Wrapped up in gloom
Pinched in their noses.
Only that little devil,
The old man's favorite,
Calls to her and points to grandpa
In the hearse:
—Sweetheart, we're coming up!
Uncle Max pull her back
He'll buy her an ice cream cone
When the ride is over.

Carica di fiori
L'altare ricoperto per lo sposalizio
Della nipote del Ministro
Che aspetta fuori da mezz'ora.
La famiglia tutta ringrazia
Per la casa
La macchina
Il vino in cantina
La pensione e la villa in Portofino—
Anche Leonardo si consola.
Gli abiti del padrone certo saran sui
Più trentamila lire e la borsa di pelle blu.

High mass in a burst of sun and flowers
The altar decked out for the wedding
Of His Excellency's niece
Who's been waiting for half an hour already.
The family is so grateful
For the house
The Mercedes
The cellar stocked with vintage wines,
All the insurance and the summer house in Portofino—
Even Lennie smiles.
All the suits are his,
A nice little sum too
And the blue leather briefcase.

3. *"Spogliarello Go-Go"*

Viene con bimbe e vecchiarelle
La nostra tanto cara tanto bella.
Capo chino in chiesa, bada,
Senza parlar vi prego!
Ecco il velo di pizzo bianco
Alla francese
L'abito nuziale con collo alto
Le mani giunte
Sul rosario madreperla—
La nonna mormora qualche parola,
Il babbo fa un cenno con la testa,
La mamma piange. . . .
Quanto sei bella piccina mia!
Senza l'incubo dell'inferno
Passi con trenta l'esame
Con lode per quel sorrisino
Che fa impazzire. . . .
Ma sù, ora basta!
Il velo, l'abito, le scarpine. . .
Sù, basta, Tesoro mio,
Non più, ti prego!
Perchè vuoi toglierti
Quelle manine bianche
Quel bel visino
Le guancie gli occhi
Anche quei piedini—
Rivestiti, sù, o muoio anch'io!

3. *"Go-Go Strip"*

Here comes our little girl
Old women children close behind.
Remember now, you bow your head in church,
No talking either!
What a lovely veil, imported lace,
The wedding gown high around the neck,
Her hands folded over mother-of-pearl beads.
Grandma mumbles something,
Daddy nods,
Momma cries. . . .
You look so beautiful, my love!
With hell no longer preying on your mind
You pass summa cum laude
For that tiny smile that drives me wild. . . .
But now, that's enough!
The veil, gown, pretty shoes. . .
No more, my darling,
Please, not your hands
Or that pretty face,
Cheeks and eyes
Those tiny feet—
Put everything back on
Or I'll die too!

CORO VIRIDIANO

Signora luna fiordimiele
Re sole portamosche e fiele
Tornano a braccietto dai divini prati
Ubriachi di vini prelibati.
Si sdraiano nel portone
Di casa Fiacca in Via Ottone
Ad una certa ora
Eccoli ancora
Masticando i venti
Con fastidiosi denti.
La gente stupíta
Guarda rapita
Accostandosi ogni tanto
Quasi per incanto
—Vorrebbero anche loro
Un pallido ristoro:
Ecco! il portone è nostro,
Tornate al prato vostro!
Poi si zuffano impauriti
Da quei vecchi inferociti. . . .
C'è una morale infatti
Ma per bambini e matti
—Che c'entrano poeti tristi
Loro, supremi egoisti?

CHORUS A LA VIRIDIANA

Madam honeyflower moon
Royal sun-carrier of flies and bile
Are back again from outings simply divine
They come arm in arm
A bit tipsy from vintage wines
Stretch across the entrance
Of Weak house on Brassy Street
Hours later still chewing the winds
With rotten teeth.
Others stare
Come up closer
Drawn by a kind of spell
—They'd like a pick-me-up as well:
Hey, you guys! This is our place
Yours is out there somewhere!
They push and shove
Frightened by those old geezers
Who come at them with their fists. . . .
There's some kind of lesson here
But for kids and loonies
—What have poets to do with time and space
They, the greatest of all egotists?

IL CENTOVENTUNO

Al sole di mezzogiorno
Sembianze care stese lungo la strada
Al fumo voluttuoso di macchine
  Ricomincia la tosse asmatica

    Ed i vecchi sdraiati al pranzo di mosche
    Ed i morti che pretendono di aver finito
con il bucato mortale
    Ed i bambini che gridano
come se fosse quell'incrocio il capolinea. . . .

Quì, ecco, finisce la salita
Per scaturire giù in curve
E la discesa che porta al rettofilo
E la stazione poi la piazza
Dove s'imbocca l'autostrada
Che va quì o là —
    (che differenza fà?)
    Pompeii una volta all'anno basta,
    Salerno oramai m'è antipatica,
    Roma è casa, già,
    ma il papa mi benedisce da lontano,
    Firenze fa il sangue troppo ricco,
    E Venezia mi fa sentire vecchia.

    Forse la Cina, chi sà?

121 CROSSTOWN

In the middle of the sun at noon
Shapes dear to us stretch the full length of the road
Voluptuous to car exhausts
    Our dry asthmatic cough starts up again

    And old men lying in their feast of flies
    And the dead pretending to have come full cycle
in their mortal wash
    And kids yelling the intersection into
the end of the line. . . .

The road climbs to here
Then plunges in and out of curves
Down the hill to the tram
To the square to the railroad station
Where you feed into the highway
Going there and there—
    (what difference where?)
    Pompeii once a year is quite enough,
    Salerno has become a bore,
    Rome, well it's home, yes,
    but the pope's blessing reaches everywhere,
    Florence is too rich for my blood,
    And Venice makes me suddenly feel old.

China, maybe. Who knows?

WILLARD

I owe you the chandelier
Destroyed through eyes slit
To narrow secrets
Not because you did or didn't
(Floodgates should be opened
Nothing trapped in prisms)—

I listened to your drunken Plato
Transvestite sonofabitch cop
Stealing your shoes!
You were the greater hunter
That long day, stalking lions
In your sneakers
(Not the first safari
But . . . who's counting?)
Your bathrobe was open, the belt
Trailed along the floor.
In the windows of Payne
You etched goodbye,
Your head a large stain under glass.

THE COLOR OF BLACK
(FOR RODNEY HALL)

In you it wears well, what others
Avoid for pale spring colors,
For the sesame street
Of small rounded joys—
You paint our wonder in white and
Mostly black, giving us back
In roses and thorns
A wide sweep of fragrant shadings.
Sleep is gentle in your words
Death a friendly voice.

TRANSLATION
(THE A-Z OF HOUSE PLANTS)

I think I've broken through to star shapes
Of scheffleras and straight sturdy stalks
Of mango trees, I've solved the green and purple
Veins of wandering jews.
Spider plants tell me of their thirst.
Spathiphyllum help me to decipher art.
In an archeological mood, I dig for roots
And wonder at their sprawling territory,
Old mysteries of birth.
Scales tell me of arrogant new cities on a leaf,
Mites leave powder traces
Where they build their bridges
In the crotch of green.
I listen to violets as they grow to power
Pink and purple in the hum of shade,
Philodendron build my walls.
In the north window, devil's cane
Broods about arctic wastes, keeps watch.
Quietly, without fuss, maranta and monstera
Vie for friendly space—
They don't mind my Roman rule,
Their gods are all safe in my parthenon.

COVERED BRIDGES

Once in Vermont we heard the earth
As it turned. There was a pause
A brief dread. We wrapped sandwiches
And took them to bed.

Past some invisible border, fruit to bud,
We grew to ripeness
Bruised in the quick passage.
In our borrowed kitchen we thought
Of seasons stretched out
As love could bear,
No turns, ramps, just lovely scenery
When we grew tired of our own large stare.

On a still morning, first hint of thaw,
We packed, put the key back
Under the brick by the door.
The road slippery,
The heater didn't work.
At the border we had coffee
Welcome release goodbye.

There are small wars with large voices
And every book opens with a lie—
Words read left to right facing West,
They give back mirror tricks when bodies
Sway against the shadow of our pleasure.
We laugh all ambiguities to the shoulder
Of our youth. And when they catch up
We read from right to left.
Endings steal upon us without style.

CRADLING MY YUGOSLAV FANCIES

I.
I don't know what was said about me
In official memos
Between Belgrade and Skopje.
I hope it was pleasant,
But, really, it doesn't matter.
The meal on top of the hill
Next to the old shrine (closed for repairs
At the time) was the best.
No exaggeration, I say what's mine
What I can back up with my eyes
And still smile, and our company
Was lively, full of jokes,
In perfect English.
It blends with other feasts—
The sculptor at the bottom of the road
(His shelves stocked with American cans)
He too was a treat.
Laughter like a golden thread
Held our intentions together,
Carried our inflections whole
Into place.   We ate yogurt
(Another kind of art) and recognized
The fluttering of love.

II.
Even at eight in the morning, prune brandy.
I didn't mind; got to like it in fact.
I drink Yugoslav wines now
Even here, where the ground is solid enough

And faces are familiar.
Shaped by a certain angle of the sun,
I dream Italian while speaking English.
Sometimes I can hear other sounds.
They too I have learned to love.

III.
I learned that black is not a color
But a state of soul.
Women veiled in it, from head to toe,
Stop briefly in the fields
And turn to watch strangers
Stuck in a ditch. Their eyes probe
Ask questions which I dare not answer.
We are all innocent when questioned
By persistent ghosts, our own.
They whisper in broad daylight
Where we are all vulnerable.
I listen.

IV.
Napoleon never carried food for all his men.
Some were bound to die on the road,
Some in battle.
My supplies are also less than life;
Things happen when we least are ready
For surprise, drama.
History is the meeting of vectors,
Always true, impersonal, for the victors
Grand even. I like my own memories,
Even out of sequence.

V.
God in his mercy gave us this mountain top
That road,
Settled us in this spot.
Socrates is a voice among many
And our own shouting seems best.
While sipping wine
We trace intentions on paper napkins
Coffee stains remind us of a joke.
After a while we learn to sketch
Rough maps of buried treasures.
I think of Njegos in black granite
Watching the sky we share.
The language is the same,
All contemporary.

VI.
Liars' dice was a parting gift.
The lawn retreated as the light grew dim,
Later, it disappeared as we sang
And grew dizzy waiting for breakfast.
I stumbled inside,
Just behind you.
Your back was a canvas
Waiting for my brush.

VII.
Stevenson too stopped here for cheese and wine.
It was special. But I prefer to remember
The wreaths on trees on the road,
The drive to Novi Sad,
The large afternoon in shirt sleeves

Talking about the post-war novel
And how it sliced through the map
Like this.
And the shy look on the face
Of our guide in Zagreb,
When she took us back home for a drink.
We had quarreled about politics,
Naturally; I don't remember what she said,
It was predictable. Her tired face
Was beautiful in that tiny slice
We carved out of the night.

VIII.
I bought napkins and stole a poster on the road,
I was shy and bold and slept through
One whole afternoon.
I swam and talked with editors
Under a large umbrella at lunch.
The ambassador invited us to cocktails
And in the new hotel I had a sauna.
I don't remember what was said,
But sitting here I see the faces
Across the way, and the chair
Tilts under me, on the sloping ground,
In the open, with the mountains
Looking over our shoulders.

IX.
Definition comes with the script.
It's all we need.
With it, the road is lit
And all things settle into place.

It doesn't matter who
Is chosen for the lead.

personae? But then she probes beyond, or rather be-
hind the mask; and the imaged grandeur crumbles un-
der a ferocious scrutiny which sets up a progression of
inverted grandeur, as in 'Notes on Still-Life'. . . . I love
the ability to see and understand and care, after some
potentially destructive knowledge . . . . I feel obliged to
single out her translations from Leopardi (a telling
choice) for special praise . . . . Anne Paolucci has found
such persuasive approximations, such elegant inter-
pretations for 'To Sylvia' and 'The Calm After the
Storm' that in her rendition they sound like English
poems to begin with."
GLAUCO CAMBON (from the *Introduction*)

. . . ABOUT *EIGHT SHORT STORIES:*

" . . . splendidly entertaining, with a sovereign art of the
dialogue and rare caricatural skill . . . , freshness of vis-
ion and incisive gift of style." HENRI PEYRE

"It is good to have Anne Paolucci's remarkable stories
. . . brought together in the present collection. Most of
us who know them will certainly want to read them a-
gain, and more than once. All of them are magnetic and
delightful."
HARRY T. MOORE (from the *Introduction*)

A GRIFFON–HOUSE PUBLICATION